THE UNRAVELING
STRANGENESS

BOOKS BY BRUCE WEIGL

POETRY

Executioner
A Sack Full of Old Quarrels
A Romance
The Monkey Wars
Song of Napalm
What Saves Us
Sweet Lorain
Archaeology of the Circle
After the Others

PROSE

The Circle of Hanh: A Memoir

CRITICISM

The Giver of Morning: On Dave Smith
The Imagination As Glory: On the Poetry of James Dickey
   (edited with T. R. Hummer)
Charles Simic: Essays on the Poetry

ANTHOLOGY

Between the Lines: Writing on War and Its Social Consequences
   (edited with Kevin Bowen)

TRANSLATIONS

Poems from Captured Documents (cotranslated from the Vietnamese
   with Nguyen Thanh)
Mountain River: Poetry from the Vietnam Wars (cotranslated and
   coedited with Kevin Bowen and Nguyen Ba Chung)
Angel Riding a Beast: Poems for America, by Liliana Ursu
   (cotranslated from the Romanian with the author)

THE UNRAVELING STRANGENESS

POEMS BY BRUCE WEIGL

Grove Press
New York

Published simultaneously in Canada
Printed in the United States of America

FIRST EDITION

Library of Congress Cataloging-in-Publication Data

Weigl, Bruce, 1949–
    The unraveling strangeness : poems / by Bruce Weigl.—1st ed.
    p. cm.
    ISBN 0-8021-3938-8
    I. Title
PS3573.E3835 U57 2002
811'.54—dc21   2002021468

Grove Press
841 Broadway
New York, NY 10003

02 03 04 05   10 9 8 7 6 5 4 3 2 1

In memory of George Eichi Kondo

CONTENTS

Part One

Oh, Atonement • 3

Immorality of Beauty • 5

Folktale • 6

I Waited for the Spirit Soldiers • 8

I Put a Shotgun to My Mouth • 10

My Pants • 11

The Super • 13

Nixon • 18

Hinckley • 20

Baby Crying, 3 A.M. • 21

Black-and-Tan Dog • 22

One of the Wives of God • 24

The Unknowns • 27

Nothing Else Sutra • 30

Teaching Hanh the Blues • 31

Home • 33

Part Two

Incident at Eagle's Peak • 37

Part Three

Time After Time • 45

Elegy for Myself • 47

The Thing (Part One) • 48

The Thing (Part Two) • 50

The Roads in Our Brain • 51

For A, at Fourteen • 53

My Autumn Leaves • 54

The Buddhas of the Bamiyan Valley • 55

That Towering Feeling • 56

The New Year Two Thousand • 58

After Horace (I, V) • 59

After Horace (II, V) • 60

Why Plato Left for Megara • 62

On the Event of My Untimely Death • 64

Finding Their Bodies at Home • 65

By the Suburban Swimming Pool • 67

Meeting Mr. Death • 68

Notes • 70

ACKNOWLEDGMENTS

Grateful acknowledgment, along with my appreciation for their generous support, is due to the editors of the magazines in which these poems first appeared:

The American Poetry Review: "I Waited for the Spirit Soldiers," "Home," "Why Plato Left for Megara," "The Unknowns," "Nixon," "One of the Wives of God," "The Roads in Our Brain," "That Towering Feeling," "The Thing (Part Two)," and "Oh, Atonement."

Field: "Home."

Gulf Coast: "Meeting Mr. Death," "Time After Time," and "Hinckley."

Poetry International: "Elegy for Myself" and "The Immorality of Beauty."

The Southern Review: "Folktale," "The Unknowns," and "After Horace (I, V)."

I am grateful for the continued support of Morgan Entrekin, Eric Price, and Ellen Levine. I also want to acknowledge the support of Roy Church, Robert Dudash, and Robert Beckstrom, who made it possible for me to come home.

It is the time of sundering . . .
Beneath the green silk counterpane.
                                  Hart Crane

PART ONE

OH, ATONEMENT

Through lonely motel walls
I heard that human *ah*
of pleasure from a woman
with a man.
I don't remember who I was then,
only that I was
alive again somehow,
so I sat up all that night,
grateful for whatever
noisy business they could give me,

but there was never enough,
so I entered the stream
and moved then
at my ease
with the current
and the dark
shapes of my baggage
through a winding
journey of a life
until some people
murdered the truth.

Yet this evening,
along roads
I have come home to
after the many deaths
and the many betrayals,
I can watch a giant
thunderhead
grow and form itself
like a living thing
into one corner
of our flat Ohio sky
and I can say,
This is where I'll pray.

IMMORALITY OF BEAUTY

The river where Faith drowned.
The marks her desperate fingers
gouged into the muddy bank.
Her pale hair
swept back in the cold current.
The heavy vines she tangled in
she hadn't known were there.

One sutra teaches
that beauty should never be possessed,
only encountered
so briefly
you are left with a kind of sorrow
and then let go
into nothing.

FOLKTALE

Nineteen fifty-seven: you
        remember the fins,
don't you,
        on the baby-
blue-and-white Bel Air?

        Beyond the pigeon coop of ghosts,
beyond the
        many-colored rabbits
penned for the evening
        by the *tap-tap*

of the old man's cane, you can see
        another man
through the muslin of time
        throw his baby
high into the air. Women

        scream from the porch, laughing.
Oh, the night is thick with blossoms
        from the blue plum tree,
and this man is full of liquor
        and of his own young life,

so he throws his baby boy
      high into the sky
as it is taken by evening
      irrevocably away from them
so that it seemed
      that I would not come down.

I WAITED FOR
THE SPIRIT SOLDIERS

I waited for the spirit soldiers
        in the mist-torn
nineteen sixty-seven
        year of our lord of the nothing,

while on the other side,
        my friend James Holmes
held a shotgun
        on a guard in a bank.

It was summer
        and he trembled, someone said,
as he stood there,
        stunned in his own plans.

He was not a dangerous or
        a cruel man, James Holmes,
but he needed the money
        to feed the many people

and their children
        of his family
who had come into his sweet care.
        He could have gotten twenty years,

but his story saved him:
        the taped-up heartbroken
shotgun that fell to pieces in his hands
        saved him;

how he had borrowed it
        from his cousin
on a desperate
        whim; how

no shell was chambered
        or loaded there. Someone said
his whole large body
        shook through the telling.

I PUT A SHOTGUN TO MY MOUTH

I put a shotgun to my mouth before:
a warmer feeling came, an end to nights
that never seemed to end, but opens a door
you may not want to step inside. The light's
not all we think it is; the black a place
that's more inviting every day, where
you may find yourself alone with grace,
with how it felt before the deaths. I can't abide
by words that simply decorate, or ask
that beauty only be the things inside of us,
apart from humanness, removed and pure, a mask
to cover who we are, as if the heart
exposed would be too much to bear. We hide
so many fears inside, so many lives.

MY PANTS

I lost some weight
until one day my pants fell down

and I felt like a little boy,
only my heart was old,

and my bloody soul
was older yet

because it had remembered,
mercifully, what the body could forget,

and because of the ghostly
company that it kept.

What are you going to do?
You lose some weight

and your pants won't stay up,
and now, and now,

I find some happiness and pleasure
just mowing my lawn

in the twilight.
I love to make the lines

straight, and breathe in
the musty sexual smell

of new-mowed grass.
I don't know

where the little boy
whose pants fell down

lives now, but it must be
somewhere in my skull,

rattling around
like a bullet, or like a scream.

THE SUPER

I met the super
on the battleship-
gray-painted
stoop
of the five-floor walk-up,
MacDougal Street, back
when it was neighborhood
and I'd
hooked up with a woman
who had money
from her folks and a job
that paid good
and who told me,

Come stay with me, honey, that
nearly forgotten summer
in the postwar
black grief and loss, and
all I had to do was
sleep up there
on the fifth floor with her and
love her some nights.
We ate dinner together in restaurants.

But that first morning
I got there ahead of her
and met the super
on the stoop
on MacDougal Street. I
was twenty. I
had already seen
inside the storm of shit,
and this woman
said with a nasal screech
that she was the super and
that I couldn't get in
nohow, as it wasn't my place,
and she called some Puerto Rican
young men to her aid
when I barely resisted
in defense of my
stupid rights
and of the rights
of the not-yet-arrived
woman who expected me, she
expected things of me if
I were to get this walk-up

room to write in or
no, I never wrote, I couldn't
write when I heard her
breathe at night so close,
although there was some
loveliness there too, I recall.

The tough guys said
they'd cut my fucking
heart out if I didn't
leave the super alone and
get the hell back
to wherever
I was supposed to be,
a question, I believe,
they had no idea
how to answer. I know
that I didn't. Later,
when the would-be
keeper of me
finally showed up,
the super relented, and
later still,

once summer
had become something
we could both bear,
we got to talking
one evening on the stoop.

August nighttime traffic and
lovers I watched, unworthy,
and in the middle
of the super's
winter story about
how the heat went off
one night in the place
so she nearly froze and
so dragged her chair
to the gas stove's
open door, propped
her tired feet there, and
fell hard to sleep, she
lifted her dress
to show me. Like you
I could hardly believe the
scars on her legs from

where they'd caught fire,
open sores still oozing
that human acid, and this
eight months after the fact.
Give us back our lives, I say.

NIXON

Everyone hated him,
and that
brought us all together
at the loins and
philosophically.
One couple among us

kept a wolf
penned in their backyard
that paced fitfully
every time I saw it,
and that never looked at you
in the eyes, although

that's not important
except for the way
that the maddening penned-up
wolf is a detail,
as in a painting,
of the lives we imagined

those nights
we would come together
to smoke

and to talk about
Nixon,
whom we had seen

in all of his flesh,
standing
on the White House balcony,
Apollonian
above the half-million
citizens who had come

to stop his killing; he
even waved to us, or
maybe it wasn't him, maybe
it was a stand-in look-alike or
one of those
cutout presidents

with a mechanical arm
that waves. Anymore
the anniversaries of the deaths
are so many
that there is little time
for anything else.

19

HINCKLEY

People wait for vultures,
who arrive
all spring morning long,
singularly
and then in pairs
and then in small groups
like black V's against the white sky,
or like lilies
opening in that
pond I can't bloody remember,
as if our lives
had some kind of wings.
Take this hand, stranger,
outstretched to you;
take these lilies;
take this vulture's air.

BABY CRYING, 3 A.M.

I've heard that hungry cry before. I know
it's hard to take sometimes, an aching, deep
abiding need to fill that human hole,
our birth and strange inheritance, the leap
into a space expanding as we breathe
it in. The mother's up. I see her through
the lamp-lit window's glare, her silhouette received
by other people's rooms and arms, those ghosts who fool
themselves and won't let go. The baby cries
until the humid black-lit street is changed.
We'll never be the same again. Our eyes
won't close as easily, our nights arranged
around the hungry cry that comes in waves.

BLACK-AND-TAN DOG

I hit a black-and-tan dog
with my car,
at night on a windy road
at 50 mph.
Thump, thump
was all that it said, sitting
strangely in the middle of my lane
like a suicide,
and it saw my eyes
in a moment
that I didn't want to
have with him,
so the next morning I drove back
to find who owned the dog,
and to say my grief
under gray autumn clouds
that hung so low
they seemed to want me. We
shift around from thing to thing
inside our minds. The geese
have come to rest
all over these cornfields.
There are so many,
like a blanket, but

no one home at the farmhouse,
where there's a bloodstain
in the road near the driveway
where the dog must have landed,
or where they had dragged it
earlier in the morning, and
stuck in the weedy ditch nearby
a homemade wreath of wildflowers
bound with a wire.
No one else in the car had seen the dog.
I was driving too fast.
It was sitting in the middle of the road.
There was no chance for me to stop.
I've played it over in my mind more than once, and
there was no chance for me to stop.

ONE OF THE WIVES OF GOD

I know what distant sirens mean;
already they have
come and passed me for another.
I know dismantlement.

Up until the moment they come for you,
it is always for another.
Sister Mary Catherine
taught me that in catechism

Father held on Saturdays
for kids who couldn't pay
for Catholic school,
so learned the rites

of beautiful suffering
from a missal,
and from Sister, sweet,
who was my

light of spirit and my Holy Ghost
and who,
in my unholy imaginings,
lifted me

above the ordinary
into condemnation.
In the pew I sat upright,
but didn't hear the Father's

words except their drone
beyond the indeterminate
boundaries of my stupor
for Sister Mary, not yet twenty,

her eyes
the still blue pond of all of my longing;
the way she
smiled down on me

a warmth that must have been the soul.
So I found ways to see her when I could,
pretending there was something

that I hadn't understood, and once
in my swoon for her body
that I could somehow feel,
even through the habit's shroud,

I wandered, drowsy,
into the house
where the wives of Jesus slept
and lived their secret lives,

and I saw her,
lit by a small lamp,
through a crack
in the wooden door.

THE UNKNOWNS

If only
they had told us
        that it was all a metaphor,
I might have learned;

        I might not have
troubled so long tonight
        over equations
my daughter

        had brought home from school; her mother
gone somewhere, and me
        her only chance at the quantities.
When I ask her

        if she thinks there are numbers
to measure loss,
        or to measure grief,
she wonders out loud

        what we would do with those sums,
once we had untangled them
        from their drowsy abstractions.
Mr. Brown

was my teacher
of the sums in the sixth grade
        and he saw the beautiful
figures in everything,

        so he
grieved over my unlearning,
        cudgeled me daffy
with his slide rule,

        and took on as his fate
my crummy well-being.
        I wanted to please him
so I cheated more than once,

        although that was neither the new
nor the old math,
        only a thing I had imagined
I invented.

        I cheated, and I copied,
and I asked some girls
        to do my work
so I could watch the grief

leave the face of Mr. Brown
when I showed him my solutions
        that were mine only in abstraction,
only because I possessed them.

NOTHING ELSE SUTRA

We were sleeping among the topiary
   in a foreign land
I had come to love
   like my own mind.

We were street-smart and jiving
   to the newest beats
up Broadway in Queens
   where they finally made the sleeping beast

arise that was the people's voice.
   We were walking on water
in the harbor
   where the ex-burning river

emptied itself,
   making a crackling,
lonely sound
   beyond the ore boats

drifting past us,
   their tiny men on deck
waving or warning us away,
   nothing else.

TEACHING HANH THE BLUES

Some things come
        simply for the sake of
goodness. A little

C, F, and G
        with the left hand
and a C-minor

scale with the right
        may take you
back to the ages

whose blood we are. Her
        fingers are strong and she's
eager to learn

how to play
        in a way
she already

understands means
        outside of herself. My
river,

I called her
        first on the streets of Hanoi
when the city's

lights had gone out
        and I'd
lost our way back home

until she pulled me
        shyly by my hand
to our dark room.

This is what I think about
        to play it like I feel,
I tell her.

HOME

I didn't know I was grateful
    for such late-autumn
        bent-up cornfields

yellow in the after-harvest
    sun before the
        cold plow turns it all over

into never.
    I didn't know
        I would enter this music

that translates the world
    back into dirt fields
        that have always called to me

as if I were a thing
    come from the dirt,
        like a tuber,

or like a needful boy. End
    lonely days, I believe. End the exiled
        and unraveling strangeness.

PART TWO

INCIDENT AT EAGLE'S PEAK

All morning long in the rain,
      I drove through the streets of my boyhood
past the falling-down houses,

with my friend from my boyhood
      who is a man now, like me, or
who lives inside of a man's body.

And after the rain stopped
      we parked the car
at the edge of a woods

that had been our
      secret place,
but where now

the county had constructed
      an asphalt trail,
wound like a scar

through what had been our perfect world,
      undisturbed by adults,
ordered peacefully by a code

that children had made up
        through all the years of children.
We walked down the asphalt trail

no longer sure of our way
        until it curved toward the river
and crossed an old path

still visible in the tangle of years,
        and without speaking
we climbed under the fence

and followed the path to the river,
        that's called the Black River,
where we swam without our clothes

in the long summers of our spirit bodies,
        and not out of nowhere exactly,
but more out of the river,

I heard my friend's voice
        rise up above the wind
and say that his life had come to nothing.

His sadness filled the air around us.
       It rose up and moved the branches.
It floated along the river like a mist,

so I wanted to find a way
       to tell him that he was wrong.
I wanted to make a story for him

that could be alive in the place
       he had come to imagine was nothing,
but there was no use for words there,

and when he had finished
       telling his long sadness,
he breathed deeply,

and he shook his head
       no to the river,
or to the wind in the trees

that makes a sound like all of memory,
       or to the life he felt strangled by.
In the distance that our eyes found together,

just at a bend in the river,
        two great blue herons
lifted and then settled again,

like silk scarves
        among the rocks in fast water.
I wanted to believe that the beauty

meant something to my friend
        in a way that could
ease the sharp hurt of his knowing.

I wanted to believe
        that he had not wasted his life,
that there was something

just in the living of it,
        hard and with some
simple human grace

that had to make it matter,
        but I didn't know
if the moment meant anything at all,

and I had to stand very still
        to try to gain my balance,
to find the rope of words that,

real or not,
        binds us to the world
and blesses us

with that sense of being
        we may imagine is a life.
And then we were walking away,

in the rain that had started again.
        We could still hear the water
rush over rocks

that had been big enough once
        to lay our bodies out across
those years ago in the sun,

and the sound the water made for us
        as we turned off the path for home
was like a promise

I remembered from before.
　　　You can tear the life out of a man
with only a few wrong words.

You can break a man's life down
　　　as if it were nothing,
just by turning away.

PART THREE

TIME AFTER TIME

You may cradle my honey whimper
       in your fresh bite.
You may shoo away the dogs

       and hush the howling
in your brain,
       but you may not forget

the boys we had been,
       and how we
promised ourselves

to each other
       in the timeless
green place by the river

that day the one boy,
       who was you as the girl,
was called through a portal

to vistas troubled
       ungreen by some voices
of the old kind,

and how the me,
who was the other boy,
            turned away and then

turned back to find you,
            my brother lover,
gone behind the time

            after time gauzy veil
don't tell me will lift;
            don't throw me a spar

or bring me the fresh cut
            flowers of the dead.

ELEGY FOR MYSELF

When they said,
You with the stars in your eyes,
I didn't know they were talking to me.
I thought it was just
voices I was hearing
in the slag heaps and
down the ethnic alleys
of stolen plums and black cherries
of late summer.
I thought it was something
wrong in my head
when someone died back then,
waiting for the flowers to blossom.

THE THING
(Part One)

I've stayed up nights
waiting for that
thing I could hear
pacing in the thicket

of cruel thorns
until the black sky
tells it that it's time
to come and get me.

Few are as faithful as I am
in their waiting.
Sometimes,
I even imagine

I can see the thing
standing in the dim
streetlight wash
in the shape of one of the lost,

one of the unloved,
forced to wander the lonely dark.
I have waited up
all night so many times for him

that I have blurred the boundaries
of good sense,
and still the thing never comes;
it always never comes.

THE THING
(Part Two)

I was
waxing nostalgic, remembering
the days of Freud,
when we still had

hope that we could drive the bad cells
out with clever talk and good intentions,
all for a c-note an hour. We believed
we could fix a bad thing

inside of a man those days;
we hadn't yet
run out of others to blame
for the mad blood we left in our wake

like a twisted offering
through the thousand years,
the pious self in us
curled up in fear

away from the unforgiving.
I was dozing and dreaming on the
rented veranda's rented
sofa in the cross-fire troubled sun.

THE ROADS IN OUR BRAIN

I believe that most folks
hide inside of a private place
where it feels like
no one can see you,

where you can shape
a small center of a thing
around yourself,
and though it isn't the real life,

we have rivers here
that run hard and cold in the spring
over limestone rocks
old as God.

I believe
that most folks
can at least imagine how it feels
to practice goodness,

if only inside of that
center that we shape around us
and imagine it's a thing
others can see.

You could
hold yourself up
against the starry sky there
and not feel a thing.

FOR A, AT FOURTEEN

You think your life is hard right now; so cold
the world seems, without much understanding.
You hurt enough to let the hard words go.
I know enough to let them ride. The thing
you have inside of you I had inside
me too. It's like you're pulled by every heart,
by every weary, needful stranger's eyes.
There isn't time enough for me. The dark

won't let me hold you, as I know I could.
We need at last a life without the grief
we've brought into the house. A life that would
allow us both our tenderness, our pain released,
the manliness for once at rest; at rest
those spirits lost, those spirits now are blessed.

MY AUTUMN LEAVES

I watch the woods for deer as if I'm armed.
I watch the woods for deer who never come.
I know the hes and shes in autumn
rendezvous in orchards stained with fallen
apples' scent. I drive my car this way to work
so I may let the crows in corn believe
it's me their caws are meant to warn,
and snakes who turn in warm and secret caves

they know me too. They know the boy
who lives inside me still won't go away.
The deer are ghosts who slip between the light
through trees, so you may only hear the snap
of branches in the thicket beyond hope.
I watch the woods for deer, as if I'm armed.

THE BUDDHAS OF
THE BAMIYAN VALLEY

I do not grieve the Buddhas
blown to pieces in Bamiyan.
It does not matter
that fifteen hundred years before,
people lived in caves
and carved the Buddhas
into the face
of the unimaginable mountain
with such exquisite care
it hurt to see.
I do not grieve for the Buddhas
blown to smithereens, pieces
smaller than your hand.
Someone thought that it would matter,
but if you blow the Buddha
into tiny pieces,
you blow nothing into pieces.
This is what they did not understand.

THAT TOWERING FEELING

I know a man
who believes he deserves to be loved
in this
loveless little village of a world.

Tonight, snow is general
all across this
new spring evening
as he tells me

on the phone
of this theory.
He is alone again
among his

money and his things.
Even those who
ruined him as a child
with their big hands and their

unspeakable preschool games
have crossed over.
We believed once
that the places

they had torn inside him,
like bat-wing
razor marks against the sky,
would grow back in the light.

THE NEW YEAR TWO THOUSAND

O holy snow,
the dogs have pissed upon you;
you are the snow
we have waited for so long.

Fast may the ice
stay far beyond our doorway,
light where we leave
and where we come.

God bless these dogs
who trot across our borders,
wild in the moon
under windows where we sleep.

Long may these days
stay drowsy
in their tempo,
sweet as they sing our way home.

AFTER HORACE (I, V)

I wonder what skinny, sweet-smelling boy
        holds you, tangled
in the roses of your unreal garden.
        Although you tie your blond hair

back with such lovely practiced grace,
        he will grieve at your moods to come;
in stunned surprise he will stare
        at the darkening waters that you trouble.

Because he thinks you are his alone,
        for him you are the light;
to him you seem content,
        the way you seem so real to the pitiless boys

always on the verge of you.
        I wrote my prayer on the temple wall.
I hung my dripping clothes to dry
        and bowed to the gods of the sea.

AFTER HORACE (II, V)

She is not strong enough yet
      to carry the wife's
double plow on her neck,
      or to bear the force of the bull's weight, pounding.

She thinks only of her ghostly fields
      where she burns back the sun's
sultry light
      in the shallows

and runs through the marsh grass unfolding.
      But don't taste those unripe grapes
until they are dappled purple
      by autumn,

until they are clustered in their true and dark light.
      Wild in his work,
Mr. Time will give her
      all of the days

that he will take from you,
      but she will want even more
than the one whose white neck
      shone like the moon on night sea,

more than the clever, fey visitor
      whose hair and sweet boy's face
baffled the girls around him
      gathered to ask him his sex.

WHY PLATO LEFT FOR MEGARA

Imagine your old teacher
        has died
in the gray broken
        columns of pious script

as he calculated
        the weight of his loss,
the unbribed jailer
        only a shadow,

like the law
        was only a shadow
that the teacher had exposed
        to the nagging light

of being
        someone. Imagine
that your name
        is not uncommon

among Greeks,
        so you must keep moving,
because he who knew all
        has passed

into the never,
       into the right understanding
of the soul's revenge
        on the body, into the justice.

ON THE EVENT OF
MY UNTIMELY DEATH

Let the fires of sweet redemption
burn my tired body into ash,
and spread that ash
among the limestone boulders
old as God
in the cold waters of the Little J
below the spired Presbyterian church.
You may even want to wet a line there,
especially in late May
where I caught my first great
brown trout on a caddis
trailed lovely by its delicate emerger.
Thank God I let that fish go.
It swam upstream and away,
then turned into a spirit
that promised many fish to come.
Sunder my ashes there.

FINDING THEIR BODIES AT HOME

A solitary dove
      came to rest in the dying willow
just as the dusk was rising,
      a detail, which in itself

was meaningless
      until the dove came back
a second time
      to the willow,

dying of omens,
      and I thought I saw
dark shapes slide by
      in the light between the branches.

I thought I saw the wings
      of a dubious angel,
so I forever keep my guard,
      and like you,

I waited for the dove to come back
      as long as the light allowed,
and then I waited in the dark
      so that my eyes took on

that different seeing,
        until I felt the breath and songs
of things who come out in the dark,
        their bodies drifting all around me.

BY THE SUBURBAN SWIMMING POOL

For one whole night and most of
all the next day,
the little dog was missing,
its people
worried about the lowering temperatures.
Two other dogs,
who I believe were
close friends of the missing,
clicked their nails
back and forth
across the tile floor in worry.
Posters were distributed
among the neighbors
and tacked to light poles
up and down the streets.
I had no rights in the matter.
I didn't even know the little dog
or why he had run away,
but he must have had his reasons.

MEETING MR. DEATH

You could say I
kept my cool
when I met Mr. Death.
I even made him
laugh
by offering my
hand to shake
in the bullet-torn
morning hours,
and then I said,
Are you looking at me?
and he got the joke. Death
gets the joke
or else
our whole lives
are a lie and a waste.
He didn't take my hand,
but he laughed at my jokes
and he made me feel
welcome inside the grace
he still wore,
shawl of the ghostly
angel he had been
but could not remember.

Mr. Death,
he was hanging around some
pals of mine, some
boys of the unspeakable
rapture of war. He
could have had me that morning
too, when I looked away
to the monsoon-heavy
river
where the bodies
had come to rest
in the last eddies,
but he changed his mind.

NOTES

Part One

"Immorality of Beauty" is for Nguyen Ba Chung (a thousand bows).

"Nixon" is in memory of President Richard Milhous Nixon.

Every spring in Hinckley, Ohio, people gather to wildly celebrate the annual return of the vultures.

Part Two

"Incident at Eagle's Peak" is for Richard O.

Part Three

"Time After Time" was inspired by the lines "you may cradle my honey/whimper in your fresh bite," from Camilla Rose, in a letter.

"That Towering Feeling" is for Toby.

"After Horace (I, V)" and "After Horace (II, V)" represent unforgivably liberal translations of two Horatian odes.

"By the Suburban Swimming Pool" is for Jack Myers.

"Meeting Mr. Death" is for Tim O'Brien.